Six Nines

Peter Langston

Copyright © 2015 Peter Langston. All rights reserved.

Peter Langston asserts his right under the *Copyright Act* 1968 to be identified as the author of this work.

All rights reserved. Apart from any fair dealings for the purpose of private study, research, criticism or review, as permitted under the *Copyright Act* 1968, no part of this publication may be reproduced, stored in a retrieval system or transmitted in any form or by any means: electronic, mechanical, photocopy, recording or any other-except for brief quotations in printed reviews-without the prior permission of the publisher.

ISBN: 978-0-646-94577-4

Published by Six Nines Imagery
www.sixninesimagery.com

Also by the same author
Six Nines (2009) Kardoorair Press ISBN 978-0-908244-79-9
Head Full of Whispers (2012) Six Nines Imagery ISBN 978-0-646-57539-1
Straightening My Tie (2014) Six Nines Imagery ISBN 978-0-646-93275-0

Foreword

Good poems, like all good art, are inexhaustible: always new despite many readings; always able to surprise, delight and satisfy.

One could paraphrase Norman Lindsay's statement about the magic pudding when looking across Peter Langston's poetry: "the more you read, the more you get." Cut and come again is its nature! This is true for the content of this first publication of Peter's poems.

No common experience is ordinary when transmuted through Peter's imaginative insight and then refined by surprisingly inventive language and inescapable imagery and metaphor. Peter's art is the alchemical philosopher's stone and what he touches he adorns with epiphanic brilliance.

Peter's muse is a modern one and yet his muse is like Ariadne with her clew, by which he, the poet, explores the labyrinth of memory and brings light to the deep resounding minotaur from the depths of his mental labyrinth.

It is not a common experience to accidentally discover a poet of such mature depth, who promises so much and will surely deliver much more.

For me, in particular, I recall the comment on John Donne's poetry: "For Donne a thought was an experience, which transmuted into poetry, modified his sensibility."

Reading Peter's poetry has had much the same effect on me.

John Rummery
Teacher and gentle opener of doors.

Contents

Foreword   John Rummery 1

The Poems   10 000 Mornings 5
Be You 6
Gone 4 Years 8
A Father's Prayer 9
His Favourite Chair 10
Those That Are Left 12
When Grandma Played Piano 14
Gardener's Dreams 15
Susie 16
You 18
Shopping List 19
Depression 20
Waiting 21
Chocos 22
Why Are They Laughing? 24
Four Nice Girls 26
August 28
Honesty 29
My Girl In The Crowd 30
Losing Weight By Proxy 31
Wondering At Woolworths 32
Sleeping 34
Too Sick To Live, Too Well To Die 35
Pieces 36
A Royal Afternoon 38
Singing 40
My Lover 42
Sunday Afternoon At The RSL 44

Nullarbor Man	45
Broken (are we rolling Bob?)	46
Ask Any Dancer	47
Warning Signs	50
Safe Harbour	52
Change of Days (camping at Yamba)	53
That Mate Of Mine	54
News Day	56
Finding Home	58
Top End Morning	59
That Coldest Hour	60
Little aMiss	61
Non Scholae sed Vitae	62

Afterword
Dedication
Poets Notes
Bio

Barry Richardson	64
	67
	68
	Back cover

10 000 Mornings

Its only been ten thousand mornings.
In that fleeting passage of sunrises
I've woken to your soft breathing;
your warm curved back and cold toes;
the steady bump thump of your heart
pumping your goodness to remote places;
those short little hairs at your temple
that first betrayed grey changes;
your cheeks, red with sleep,
scaffold your first smile
and help your lips form the words
innumerable sunrises have heralded.
"I love you."
Said each of ten thousand mornings
but never once repeated
because each was said as new.
Each first-light view ignores familiarity
as you draw breath
on our reinvented love affair,
a familiar experience,
gifted to you
for yet another first time.
Every one of ten thousand sunrises
has delivered you to me, new and beautiful.
I know every arc, every curl.
I know your scent, your rhythm.
You are as familiar as the blackbird's pre-dawn call
which wakes me to watch you.
Yet despite knowledge and logic
which offers me easy assurance of who you are,
tomorrow morning
another sunrise will bring you to me
brand new.

Be You

Sun floods me
Stretching my pores until soaked,
they spill radiant leftovers
in unwasted outfall.
Page corners flutter
with the same breeze
which sings me the ocean's stories
from as far as I can squint.
The gentle blue rolls in,
bares its friendly teeth in greeting
to yellows and greens
convinced of their impenetrability.

In awe of this perfection,
amongst passions of my lifetime,
I drink it and breath it and feel it,
then think of you,
my Vivaldi daughter,
an original creation
of determination and self worth
threatened only by the same drives
that sustain her.
That genetic echo beating time
somewhere deep,
somewhere shallow.

It's mid October again
and every glisten of white on blue
might stand for a thought
in the short collection of ideas
watchers call your life.
Equally and alternatively,
each could be a time I've loved you
in smiles and tears and aching pride,
in anger and tears and frustration.
Each set remembered or forgotten
depending on viewpoint,
now spent and worthless.

Be proud, my girl.
Your journey demands it
and no matter what part I play
in answer to your direction,
make use of me while I stand.
For on wild days,
foundations save us
in the unseen work
that allows the world to wonder
your survival in all weather.
But the parts are not the whole
and you remain the architect.

Be you.

Gone 4 Years

Your lonely look followed me
to the carpark,
back to Tamworth,
leaving you scattered
among half-empty boxes
and objects d'life.
Fear and excitement polarised,
toggle switching emotions
in a room for one.
Four loving voices,
too far away
to bolster your lonely independence.

Sex, drugs, rock 'n roll,
assignments failed,
ripped off,
ticked off,
loved, hated, ignored.
Counsel sought,
counsel given.
Ecstasy and despair ...

... until age defined in its own time.
Assignments aced,
a slow heart beat to success.
Repeated lessons learned.

Today you stand so tall,
even among clever companions,
beaming me that lantern-jawed smile
before acknowledgement by acclamation.
I want to scream to the world
of your origins,
your struggles,
your victory.
To tell them we share a name
and the light and shade of life.
Should my chest burst,
blame pride and admiration
and know this is my son.

A Father's Prayer

Dear God
Thanks for my Dad:
for his patience and love.
For those talks I loved
and particularly for those I avoided
but he made time for anyway.

Thanks for this bundle in my lap.
Show me how to guide him.
Give me wisdom when he asks questions
and patience when he doesn't.
May he learn where he comes from
in order to know where he is going.

Thank you for my son.
For his straight back,
true heart
and beautiful mind.
May he learn from this bundle
as I did from him.

May I live long enough
to stand with them both
and show the world your work,
as good fathers always have.

His Favourite Chair

"It was his favourite chair" she said,
eyes floating in salty pools,
lip trembling with age or fear or both
and words spoken to plead a case.

So they worked around her,
collapsing their life into cartons
of homogenous blending
so no memories remain special.

Carefully, they hid his medals
beneath his parents gold-framed wedding,
beneath a draw from her craft room,
beneath three toilet rolls and a work jumper.

Their life reordered by a strangers' priorities
and vouched safe to ribbed cardboard
and screaming tape,
each yelp a newly stabbed pain.

"Not yet," she said to a vacant lounge room
and pressed down into worn cushions
for escape or a temporary hiding place
from the insanity around her.

As the calendar left the wall
she caught his neat, red script -
a doctor's appointment in boxed reminder.
Her mind, still sharp, counted 24 days.

Enough time to end 52 years
and find a blue-lipped companion in your bed.
Enough time to bury him
but too short a time to say goodbye.

She watched pieces of him pass by
and something of her too.
Then beds, wardrobes, cupboards,
'till reluctant hands matched shuffled feet.

"It's time," their daughter said
struggling with soft words
with the strength of a gentle touch.
"I kept this ..."

She felt the soft wool pat her thin grey hair,
smelled his hair lotion,
smiled at knitting memories
and his love of warmth and age.

She stood, turned and patted the arm rest.
"Off you go Bob."
Behind her back, it was heaved and carried
and swallowed by her pantechnicon future.

Tears mingled in each other's hair
as mother held daughter held mother
in safety's embrace.
"Oh dear. I'm so scared."

This poem was performed by the Armidale Playhouse
as part of "My Favourite Shorts", in April 2010.

Those That Are Left

Pre-dawn egalitarian silhouettes
move inward along the spokes
to a gathered mass at the hub
where iron gates of a rising sun
give lie to the darkness.

The sudden stark glare of a single floodlight
assigns rank, status and privilege for minutes only
as we engage in the social game of recognition
and accede priority to beaded caps, berets and uniform:
to clinking medals hung from colourful ribbons.

Respect offered in any way we can
we hear their humour in the ribald comment,
we accept their humanity in complaints of age
and we wince at the catalogue of their recent losses
as we stand among them, proud.

The quips and giggles flowing among them
belie butterflies lurking for what is ahead:
just as it may have been when knees responded keenly
and eyes more sharply picked dangers in the darkness.
This morning, fear of their own darkness keeps them grouped.

At the Rising Sun gates, words order us
and tell our ears of service, pride, courage, sacrifice,
whilst speaking reminders to medal shielded hearts.
We sing the Recessional as best we can
with mumbled words and in the wrong key.

At the Ode, an old man of rank struggles to stand,
legs with spokes holding him
until a straight-backed sergeant salutes assistance.
Light blue is in the sky
and blood-earned pride in their voices.

"We will remember them" a promise kept
and "Lest we forget" a warning given
to themselves as much as others.
Braced and embraced by a trumpet's Last Post
his old, frail salute honours them all.

Other ripened boot heels snap to, attending a tribute
to mates long gone but standing with them.
Some clear their throat, some sniff and one sobs
till a tender heart reassures his mate's regret.
"Me too." Eloquent permission for a hard man's tears.

And in the minute which followed
people breathed freedom and peace and gratitude and love
for strangers who didn't need to know our names
to die
and then allow us to weep with them.

We left them there in growing light,
more blue now than black.
Faces back in place
where their souls had just been
and planning *their* day.

An old lady struggled past, gait heavily dependent on stick.
Nestling a requiem of flowers: a quiet gift made annually
to a beautiful boy who gave her his name
and sixty years of longing.
She still says thank you.

Saving them till this moment,
I wept my first tears.
Confused at their origin
but not unhappy at their arrival
and awestruck at their architects.

When Grandma Played Piano

Like bones dancing in a spectral ballet,
your fingers jitter and skip
in matters of choice between black and white
and actions of independence from a taxed brain.
You remember how it was
with grimace and complaint,
unwilling to continue, unable to stop
while younger voices encourage you with singing.

Your self-effacement holds some honour
but the greater part, insecurity,
calls for strength and approval
and a long lost little girl's need for love.
Through age, infirmity, pain and embarrassment
the vaguest pilot light glows
then flickers signs of a life unfinished
as a twenty minute encore leaves us laughing ...

... and crying ...

... thanking God for gifts and mercies
great and small,
wrapped in your little bundle
of bones and occasional smiles.
A shaking finger searching in mid-chorus,
touching a dead daughter's smile.
Memories of you and us,
that must outlive death
to become legacy ...

... and on you played with faltering keystrokes
feathers sprinkling their uncertainty on lonely keys,
our voice more certain of following notes
than the following years.
Whilst music fell victim unintentionally
it offered its passengers safe journey
as love and gratitude took centre stage
when Grandma played piano.

Gardener's Dreams

We can share them.
We may even see them come true
but no one else
can have our dreams.
You taught me them,
not guilt:
love,
not shame.

Like a constant gardener,
you planted seeds,
watched them grow,
burst forth from me
as passion and love of life
and people
and ideas.
You let water and sun take the credit
your nurture deserved,
but watched your sapling dream -
your silent reward.
Even saw me writhe in nightmare -
but seasoned by familiarity with storms
and the knowledge that the worst weather
breaks only the weakest branches.
Reassuring both of us that
"This Too Will Pass".

Strong now. Confident.
A touch of my own gardener's wisdom
grafted from original oak
and able to raise seeds to saplings.
I remember first lessons
and remind them to dream,
as I still do
and will forever.

Your beautiful, evergreen gift.

Susie

Susie sat in silence
a sneaky cat eyeing her prey
high up on the lowest branch
where big sisters never climbed.

Susie came here to hide
a small window to an outside world
just outside the fence
banned by mum and dad.

Susie made the world go by
On her branch, time stood still
even in memories she's still six
innocent of wicked hearts.

Susie's eyes sparkled
Her straight-backed brother below
always alert at a sister's expense
for the chance of mischief.

Susie heard his targets complaining
Sisters who rode horses to ribbons
now did her chores too
between cries of injustice.

Susie watched her Dad
fixing this, moving that, wishing for the other.
Lessons for a little girl
from his hard day's life.

Susie heard her mother's calls
ignored all but meal invitations
feigning no responsibility over household tasks
as did the brother she worshipped.

Susie's daydreams lived on her branch.
They played with her as leaves rustled
stayed until exhausted by her possibilities,
her endless creativity

Susie's daydream journeys ended.
The dinner yell drove her down
scampering barefoot to bare boards
and the last place at the table.

Susie's father made them wait to eat
and swore them to keep the secret
of Susie's secret hideaway
a secret from Susie.

Susie smiled and ate and grew
beyond black and white moments
into the colour of a woman
but still with her Scout smile.

Susie grew into a wife
and a mum at her own table
who daubed colours on her children's worlds
and hugged life into them there.

There's beauty in smiling eyes
Windows on a generous heart
A tree, a daydream, love
and a little girl's uncomplicated joy.

Susie was a little girl once
and then forever happened
so she shared her smile
and then her daydreams

with me.

This poem was performed by the Armidale Playhouse as part of "My Favourite Shorts", in April 2009.

You

I kiss your cheek so lightly
that you feel only my intentions.
That small spot will tingle and burn
with the flush of love's acknowledgement.
My fingers reach for yours
dancing like spider's legs
gossamer touches under summer soaked sheets,
until they nest in your palm.

My chin goes adventuring across your shoulder
until my stubbled cheek finds rest
in the hollow of your neck
where sounds of heart and lungs sooth my troubles.
I hold you like a ghost
and breathe you in
your soul and mine in linked embrace
and give my life to your indulgence.

When I wake in the cold bleakness of necessity
I'll be warmed knowing your sunrise thoughts are of me
and begin my countdown in the daylight hours
until dreams bring me to you again.

Shopping List
- soluble aspirin (for my migraines)
- panadol (for your knee)
- ~~five~~ six chicken thigh fillets
- leek
- 2 carrots
- ~~cellery~~ celery
- sambol olek
- onion
- bandaids
- soy milk (the Vita stuff)
- wheatbix
- my bread
- your bread

<u>Other stuff</u>
- go to bank
- drop off xray to Dr
- have a walk
- ring your brother (please)

I'm not sure we have enough chicken so you better check (freezer)
Why don't you stay for a coffee?

Mundane lists
on a kitchen whiteboard:
links to the real world,
bridges to cross,
invitations to dance in winter sunshine
with all the world as my partner.
Written casually with apparent haste,
yet each item a knotted lifeline
only I can climb
on this dreary day.
A shopping list, personally annotated
with silent encouragement
and hidden tearful hopes
that I might grasp its knotted rope
and climb, one by one,
into the sunshine.
I'll slip but never fall:
your will prevents it,
even when I let go.
This steadfast grip of yours
my lifeline's unfailing anchor.
Uncompromising, tenacious love,
expressed in dot-point simplicity.
The lady in the coffee shop says hello …
you forgot the yoghurt …

… small victory
I didn't.

Depression

Made the bed,
cutting my line of retreat
but retreated,
defeated
anyway.
Untouched by anything
or anyone
but horrors.
I smelled like my dreams looked
and wallowed under blankets
while hours slow-motioned the morning.
I cried someone's tears,
felt their regret
and recrimination
and defeat
and shut my eyes for sleep,
a coward's suicide.
A reasonable man
with enough guilt
to share among a queue.
Debts beyond emotional resources,
creditors deserving repayment
but who can only watch
and wonder
what being me is like,
what I might have been,
if this fuck had chosen otherwise
and not blackened my soul
or gripped my heart
with its bony frozen fingers.

I wonder in return
as you watch me writhe,
what life must be like
built on scream-less dreams
and sunny days
and hope.

Waiting

Sitting in this wild place,
waiting for the news,
your spirit sings to me,
new lullabies for old fears.
I hear your mothering at water's edge
lap, lap, lapping a patient rhythm.
Comfort like a heartbeat.
Nearly gone, always there.
I see your smile dancing in the ripples
laughing reflections on the walls
sharing jokes and stories,
with me still thirsty for learning.

A soft breeze whispers your name
and you are here with me
still offering whatever you have
to raise me up
to save me.
Ever mindless of self
all offers without conditions
and courage enough to share.

Red fills rampart walls above me
glows the days fulfilment.
Waterbirds dip and dive to drink.
A cheeky moon steals some daylight kudos.
Lizards scamper for safety in the Spinifex
while the sun, floods the scene.
Closer to nature than any of fifty years
I'm still closer to my Mum tonight.

I wait for news
to say goodbye again.

Chocos

In July our Chocos stood to their knees in mud
facing a brutal bully,
outnumbered, outgunned, out supplied,
a long way from home
and a hare's breath from death.

Weeks of training in soldiering
faced thousands of samurai years
and called instead on their deeper experience,
of being Australian,
refuting their enemy with slow defiance.

The hills of home were not this steep,
the slopes not as muddy
and the trees held no machine guns.
But those ragged bloody Chocos
lay their bodies across a war machine's path.

For two long months.

General Blame Me,
of firm footing and starched uniform,
both testicles in MacArthur's hand
and kicking own goals with his mouth,
dismissed their effort.

Conscripts for mainland service
Koalas – protected and not to be shot at.
"Rabbits who run get shot" he said.
Strauss' melting Chocolate Soldiers.
A brave commander speaking from his desk

The braided caps justified their criticism
and sacked the wrong men
because bold words sounded better
spoken past a corn cob pipe.
So heat affects chocolate hearts.

400 faced 5000 on any given day,
slouch hats dipped below bullets.
The 39th Battalion – Maroubra Force
1500 extraordinary men
but only 200 stood by October.

Six hundred wooden boxes of Chocolate.
The price of freedom in 1942.
In Darwin, even cheeky sparrows hid from the parks
and in Sydney our ladies painted on stockings
and waited for Yanks.

Those slouch hats dip no more.
Below their rising brim
brown eyes birth a slow smile
and six hundred tears
wash clean their hands.

Why Are They Laughing?

Why are they laughing?
They move so slowly
in splendid white and cream.
They bend with stop-motion stiffness
and roll languid returns shyly back to the action.
They bowl like grandfathers -
a parody of younger selves -
but still shout with appealing passion.
Catches are spilled or missed or ignored
and they mull on what was.

But why are they laughing?
A total to chase, they go out now in pairs
whilst the remainder dissect the errors.
Pads with buckles and green-dimpled gloves
make louder statements than grey temples
but take their trusted place on sore legs and hands.
A quick single claims the first,
an impatient swing many more
but a few stand steady as memory serves
the best of them, best.

And they are still laughing
when play continues at the bar
and ales sooth unrealistic expectations
which had hoped for glory's return.
Here the past falls away, no longer of use.
They call to each other still
of businesses, relationships, marriages, lives
some ruined, some still flowering
and pain not shown on the field of green
lies about for mates to sort the pieces.

They find laughter still among the devastation
as a chat becomes alternate shouts
and occasional interjectors with twopence to spend.
A quiet beer lasts through singing
and the antics of the clown in every circus
until the night is spent with the exhaustion
of men talking their troubles in twos and threes.
No problems solved
but aching silent hearts given voice
lightened by mates like these.

It ends.
Stiff legged, they promise return.
Strong hands, STRONG hands,
hands that will hold you up through time and distance,
tell me they love me
while their mouths swear and issue oaths.
Legends leave for that other life
which would make them myth,
their hearts pumping for brothers,
their mouths roaring like champions.

... and they laugh and laugh and laugh
decoding years of programming
until permission only the company of mates will allow
brings anger and frustration and relief and love
closer than periscope depth.
The surface tension broken,
no murk left between hiding place and daylight,
acceptance and belonging lead them to salvation
and the real men their fathers talked of being ...
... and tears begin to fall.

Four Nice Girls

Four nice girls came past on Sunday.
Four nice girls
dressed appropriately
for their age
for my street
for the time of day
for the weather.
Dressed so that "appropriately"
would likely be called old fashioned.
Four nice girls.
One laughed because something was funny,
not because she had to.
Another said a polite hello
with no more than a sweet smile.
A third said thanks
for a wayward soccer ball's return.
The fourth said nothing
her older sister couldn't.
Four nice girls.
I had forgotten them,
lost among a lost generation
with so many choices
that it makes so few
and then,
mostly the wrong ones.
The abandoned park outside my fence
where young voices grew old
and ran for adult playgrounds,
where four nice girls
kicked and giggled and chatter-boxed innocence
long bled from this place.
Where they ran, the grass turned green
and ghosts of dogs barked children's songs
whilst four nice girls played their game,
collapsing in laughter and hugs
on a lovely Sunday afternoon
as rain washed their smiles.
I wanted to thank these four nice girls
but having learned misunderstanding's risk
to the innocence in all of us,

I chose instead to add my smile -
the happy old teacher one -
and allowed my heart to defy its chains
and thoughts to drift to simpler times
when too much fun changed your life
it didn't take it.
When children became adults
after they were ready
and young girls only carried babies
for aunties or mums
and childhood didn't end in sadness
and four nice girls
didn't look unusual
kicking a ball
in the park
on a wet Sunday afternoon.

August

She's gone away
this friend of my daughter,
this soul I'll never know
or tell my stories to
or see my wife comfort.

Yet her black curls still bounce,
her brown freckles still polka-dot
a Snow White smiling face.
She calls to me and giggles
and runs to the safety of her daddy's arms.

Little August will dim in our imaginations
but not yet, not soon.
Sometime after the pain stands in the distance
when tears can fall for other topics
and broken hearts beat safely again.

For ten weeks motherhood bloomed in my daughter,
grew manhood in another's son.
I loved them more for their growing,
roots mingled and bound only in shallow soil
no firm hold against unjust winds.

Farewell little one
The path is lit for you.
You will be led by familiar others
you have known for eternity
and they will keep you warm and make you laugh.

Honesty

Honesty has a sweet face
dressed not in uniform
or wig and gown.
Not aged by expectation
or shaped by cultural origin.
Not decreed by role
or profession
or a statement of duties.

Honesty is new on the job,
with only a basic education
but uncorrupted by complexity.
Kept fresh by simple needs:
the need for food,
for shelter,
for safety,
the need for love.

Honesty meets you with blue eyes
and maybe a some-toothed smile,
or a stormy frown
and tear-stained cheeks.
Clutching fingers,
words to showcase ignorant adults
and interest repeated
at the simplest things.

Honesty may be named Jack
or any other favoured title.
We say we treasure these
and yet we allow corruption
to wipe them clean
of their birth-given gift:
to project truth without agenda
and amplify love through honesty.

My Girl In The Crowd

You sit there smiling at the world
unafraid to let it know of your happiness.
Bravado born of experience.
A myth match of fantasy v fact.

Standing below on the concourse
Watching your eyes wander the set
and drink the moment,
unnoticed, I watch you smile.

For stolen minutes, I sup you.
The very redness of your top
clinging with pride to its foundation
before disappearing into its denim compliment.

Greying strands of hair in nature's haphazardry,
an old man's tease and young man's wonder.
Your body, full and thin in magic concurrence,
still makes suggestions even in venue seating.

And those eyes, wandering the scene
and using your smile to beam the confidence
that husband and babies and workplace and life
have gifted you as deserved compensation.

Seats fill about you, painting a human mosaic
and others jostle for my attention
like colours jealously competing on a palette,
yet my eyes still daub you first.

Here on the concourse I spy on in admiration.
I want to wave and see your smile widen for me,
but cast in your spell, I leave it smiling for you
and stand here instead, counting heart beats.

Losing Weight By Proxy

I wake to your footsteps
resonating through groaning floorboards
each wooden stretch an apology.
You sing your joy
accompanied by untuned dishes
clanking a reminder
of my incomplete task.
In the half-light at 7:00am
even the sun is reluctant
but I'm expected to rise.
"Going for a walk?'
a question your near naked appearance
left me ill-prepared for
'till you twist-turned into bra cups
and hoisted straps over shoulders
as though lace could become overalls.
"Stay there. I'll go by myself!"
is beamed at me with such enthusiasm
reality is suspended for milliseconds
and your smile coaxes my feet to the carpet
and a bridge too far.
Outer garments in place,
you carry lazy shoes to the door
as I drag along behind
on my invisible lead,
until as if by miracle
or guilt,
only minutes later
I'm throwing an apple core at a cat
halfway to the shop,
me on a milk mission
whilst you exercise.
Had I known how hard it would be
for me
while you
reached 75kg
I would have thought twice
and slept in more often.

This poem was performed by the Armidale Playhouse as part of "My Favourite Shorts", in April 2010.

Wondering At Woolworths

A woman too big for a blouse too small
I wonder what Rachel Welsh is doing?
Confused grey hairs wandering until a son finds her
I wonder what Mum is doing?
Teenage grownups swear in doubled decibels
I wonder what Snoop Dog is doing?
Two teens have, like, a dialogue, you know man
I wonder what Kylie Mole is doing?
Three others locked in discussion with mobiles
I wonder what conversation is doing?
Security skulks by, radio and dirty looks armed
I wonder what Sergeant Shultz is doing?
4 races, 7 nationalities in my field of view
I wonder what Please Explain Pauline is doing?
iPods, blue tooths, mobiles flashing, beeping, vibrating
I wonder what my crystal set is doing?
Green bags, blue bags, plastic bags
I wonder what brown paper is doing?
Jeans living on the pubic line
I wonder what teenage waists are doing?
Girls turning 21 with six year old burdens
I wonder if ten seconds was worth the doing?
No space for grandma in a room full of bums on seats
I wonder what that seat on the bus is doing?
Middle-aged couple not holding hands
I wonder how they are doing?
An old man weeping into a complementary coffee
I wonder what he'd rather be doing?
All eyes turn to a black man, tall and straight
I wonder what we should be doing?
Three farmers in school uniform tip their hat
I wonder if respect is hard to be doing?
A mother worries past, waiting for a phone's ring
I wonder what her child's been doing?
I'm watching these snap shots of lives
Wondering should I feel guilty in the doing?

Then two little boys, linked with their father's hands,
Look way up there to his eyes in the sky
and see love and feel trust and know safety
and I wonder when my little boy skin left me?

Watching these strangers parcelled in their worlds
and intersecting briefly at cash registers
I see their future as my past
and their present as my future
and I wonder.

Sleeping

12:30

                                      the house settles and joints creak
                                          the TV stares blankly at the couch
                           the dishwasher runs out of imagination
                                    she rolls and sighs her day away
                            I drift to Nod in the cacophony of silence

1:15

more saw joints crack and creak satisfaction
a dog barks, sentinel to nothing
a neighbour's car lights my window
she snores with rhythmic lungs
I take a last exhausted leak

3:30

                                only the fridge still hums its business
                                                  the air seems thinner
                                            shadows seem thicker
                                    she breathes apathy from far away
                           I cringe behind lids as the nightmares come

4:30

the house stands hushed, waiting
appliances hold their breath
ants stand still at kitchen morsels
she has deserted me for dreams
I wake in wide-eyed fear

4:35

breathing strangled breaths
eyes darting for dangers
seeing only replayed images
she shuffles off to a closed lid
I struggle on with borrowed heartbeats

5:07

                                  the computer hums familiarity
                                  in chorus with the electric jug
                                a car hurries by without looking
                                    she rolls again, chasing dreams
                                    I chase reality in a clean kitchen

5:43

birds sing their brave pre-dawn songs
as the first dim colour evicts the night
a garbage truck is injustice of the peace
she blows hay from a fevered nose
I keep counting minutes

Too Sick To Live

I am not dying:
statement of belief,
lacking confidence
to make it fact.
Adhesive dots in elbow joints.
Blinding pinpoints in my eyes.
Inflating cuffs on short sleaves.
Beeping temperate probes in my ear.
Piss in a bottle.
An over friendly doctor
explores the inner man,
starting at the end.
I should have bought flowers.
Such unnatural acts
of science and medicine,
to prove my physical health
and undress the mental
and leave it naked
in the waiting room.
Six months of data
and worry,
when a dedicated listener
would do.
I'm not dying,
... I just want to.

Too Well To Die.

Pieces

She sits before them
or them before her,
slowly emptied
like a Russian puzzle

          pieces
          just pieces
          all she has
          all she wants
          all she trusts
          pieces
          of the past
         gathered too young
         before too late
       crumbs under old tables

from yellowed envelopes
small ring boxes
old age folded
in tissue paper

          pieces
          to reform
         with clever hands
          sharp eyes
          open mind

covered in old memories
of lives once lived
but now in pieces
in an old shoe box.

          pieces
          priceless
          unique
          links
         membership
          pieces
         of an old canvas
          jig-sawed
          scattered
         to hide a past

Arms encircling
lest a breeze might finish
what years have tried,
she picks at familiar pieces,

          pieces
          of ghosts
       daring a compositor
         to release them
        from gossamer cells

births, death & marriages,
painting faces on skeletal names
canvassing canvasses
long abandoned

                                                       pieces
                                               of how it is
                                           not how it was
                                        fragments through
                                          family cataracts
                                                     pieces
                                           with no context
                                       meaning misshaped
                                            edges blurred
                                          to fit any truth

and that hardest truth,
changing stories to fact,
speaks clearly to her
for those that follow,

                                                   pieces
                                            put away
                                       in wrong boxes
                                            illusions
                                      of good old days

whilst whispers
float off
asking for forgiveness
honour for their death.

                                                   pieces
                                            put away
                                       in wrong boxes
                                           illusions
                                     of good old days
                                                pieces
                                         of blue sky
                                        or blue tales?
                                     red poppies dancing
                                 or bloody, deadly sins?

Moved and instructed,
it's as good just to bathe,
to wash in these memories
and belong,
until tears dry.

                                                   pieces
                                         just pieces
                                       of other lives
                                             her life
                                     restless to leave

A Royal Afternoon

Under the fancy sails
where no boat has ever been
in a garden where only beer grows
and with thoughts as my only chums:
sitting, en plain air at the Royal.
Spring Ridge settles at my sleaves.
Black soil plains run away to Gunnedah,
the vision splendid
a vision-filtered
by silky oaks
and passing B-Doubles.
Flies join me for a beer
but refusing to shout
they sip away at mine,
some of them preferring to swim.
I wave them off,
more landing instructions than deterrent.
Four Gold X's slip past lips
Forced by bloke manners
to break the silence
and "g'day" a blue singlet
who passes like Treebeard,
all loud footfalls and subhuman grunts
'till he nods a reply.
Words crawl across the white space
like blue and khaki wandering in
as if their first time
in a place reverence.
Adjusting quickly,
they swill and fill
cold beer sold for dusty throats
and dry arguments.
Always the restless watcher,
words spill again
across insatiable lined blankness,
until stopped by a sore wrist..

They look up from the page,
pause,
shine awhile,
as bright in my eyes
as they sparkled in my soul
before my midwife duties birthed them
to be nurtured and read,
trusted now to others
that they may raise them.

Another sip under the sails.
"Get home, ya mongrel!"
sends a dog packing
and me reaching for car key assurance
as the air gets thick
and the day old
with oft-repeated oaths
of sex and genitalia.
The plains are gone,
replaced by a black backdrop
hung with trucks and truckies,
utes and farmers.

Shouts about shouting
as conversations become direct.
An author who knows his audience,
I leave,
before a man
alone
writing
threatens the bar.

Singing

I hear singing
mental chattering
drowned
replaced
by singing.
Beautiful Singing.
Zimmy said it best:
I turned and she was
standing there
singing
with silver bracelets
and flowers
asking me questions
interested in my answers
and singing
with her eyes
and her imperfect smile
so perfect
I couldn't leave it
or the singing.
My heart beat
it must have
intoxicating rhythms
somehow I knew
the singing
was a warm blanket
safety from
hazy black shades
of mental winters

singing
happy tunes
of infrequent rhymes
and three more smiles
like hers
singing
a future
and a past
I could live with
belong to
singing
me home
she took my crown
threw it in the street
started something
started singing
with angels' voices
I danced to the tune
rested in the lyrics
gave myself to her song
singing
as she left
smiling our future
with a promise
of a second verse.

My Lover

That certain smile of yours
starts in small cracks
but never breaks your whole face open
taking its preferences
somewhere between rhymes:
sly and wry.

It's a signal.
No clanging bell
or flashing light:
subtly part of the presentation
and challenge,
like watching a passing season.

Then your fingers are like feathers.
The lightest cool wafting that warms.
Sleight of hand to the back of mine,
then neck, then face.
Soon promises touch my lips
through your silent, gentle fingertips.

Soon we are all soft skin and orange glow
as our clothes lay in careless pools,
a camouflage skin of who we become
protecting who we really are.
Naked in each others' arms
we are never better dressed.

We track new paths over well known ground.
Breathing, touching, holding, kissing,
like first-time lovers,
in wonder and discovery
and disbelief that intimacy
is never bored with its memories.

In the comfortable tangle of aftermath
our only words are of love,
knowing this act is a touchstone
for the laughter, the beauty, the growing,
the tears, fears, years,
of wanting no one else.

I think on this as you doze
and your fearless heart beats
a conundrum of gentle love and strength
against my resting head
and a breath, a smile and a tear
ease their contented way from me.

Sunday Afternoon At The RSL

A juke-junk four piece pounds on deaf ears,
which hear only static even aided
under perms or bald patches
at the local RSL.
Years hide behind vacant looks
telling the same old stories
of disapproval
disagreement
disenchantment
with young people
who have their own teeth
but no manners.
Was it Jim or Van
Who once lit their fire?
Coals burn cold and black,
no smoke, no fire, no music,
since Don pronounced it dead.

He returns from the bar,
tray of beers balanced in his right hand
walker pushed with his left,
not a drop spilled
and dignity intact
but his world shrunken as far
as two shuffling feet
and four small wheels
can take you.
No news beyond the letterbox.

Nullarbor Man

Bare arms strain the tolerances of short sleaves
Black, primate hairs thick coat the skin
Hands hang like the Babe's leather mitt
Shoulders turn sideways for doorways
A Nullarbor man.

Conversation uncommitted, but friendly
"How's the travelling" drops out.
He needs no closure on this casual loop.
He knows rhetorical without spelling it
this Nullarbor man.

Barely smiles for friends, never for strangers
Ancestors rolled durries at the stock camp fire,
drank sweet black tea and stared at embers.
Held single word conversations.
"Yep" a Nullarbor man.

This modern plainsman moves people
manages their comforts without pandering
Civil, taciturn, reasonable, direct, accepting fools
Stupid questions returned with a considered yes or no
Nullarbor man.

Every day the same as the surrounds
Same travellers, same problems, same complaints
Fix a tyre, give directions, ring a till, make a coffee
Same mates, same women, same small bed at night
Nullarbor man.

Dull, empty eyes fixed on distances beyond flat horizons
to the same places, the same comforting tedium
"The money's good mate – why ya wanna know?"
Groundhog day as a life choice
for a Nullarbor man.

What's he thinking?

Broken (are we rolling Bob?)

broken bottles
broken glass
broken rules
broken speed limits

broken road
broken fences
broken signs
broken letter box

broken roofs
broken windows
broken swing
broken street lights

broken cars
broken engines
broken bikes
broken windscreens

broken faces
broken limbs
broken hands
broken shoulder blade

broken notes
broken abstinence
broken future
broken truth

broken homes
broken promises
broken lives
broken dreams

broken smiles
broken trust
broken innocence
broken child

broken spirits
broken down
broken open
breaking point

Broken Hills on a Lightning Ridge
everything is broken.

Ask Any Dancer

Reliving his old age -
youth previously abandoned -
he rocks more than rolls
wary of the wheels
rolling might bring.
Disgracefully channelling Ray
or Little Richard
or Electric Bob from Minnesota
he could be knockin' on heaven's door
but not yet.
Not in the first set.
Band's hot,
room' jumping
red blood surges
to forgotten places
confusing the unemployed
into panic.
Yeah,
I say yeah,
I say yeah!
'till he opens his eyes …

… the dance floor lies empty,
polished parquetry shimmers
in red and blue and green
calling dancing shoes out
from homes watching the football.
Sweaty young things,
just ghosts in mini skirts
who bump and grind their lust.
only if you squint to the beat.
Instead, granny substitutes
tap their toes and smile
at urges who linger
in the Rock 'N Roll,
then lapse,
spilled on sweaty memories
even he can't kiss to life.

In a pimpled corner,
young men drink and mock,
safe in shadows as watchers are:
little moths drawn to Fender flames
and rasping vocals
and primal beats on skins.
They laugh at age-defying acts
of middle-aged dancers.
Watch their next thirty years
boogied before them,
too drunk or scared or stupid
to see the painful truth in their jests.

The beat goes on
and on and on ...
'till there in lights
all rock-coloured highlights
over experienced contours,
she is there,
moving,
eyes down, hands up,
surrendering to the groove.
Swaying hips,
gene-jeanie-tight bum,
low cut top,
high cut cheekbones.
Teenage info
in an adult data base.

The guitarist smiles.
On keys, fingers twitch
whilst drums and bass just play,
that's what they do.
At the microphone,
words are stumbled over,
too many thoughts at once
when she turns
and smiles
what Mona Lisa thought.
Fresh groomed wet lips,
wet and smacked,
part at the idea of him
but soon retreat,
aware of time
and opportunities
lost.

Little boys sip in silence
not knowing what to do,
even if given the chance,
but catch a glimpse
of manhood's rewards.
Smiles and shudders coincide.
They could be watching their mother.
"Enjoying it way too much dude."

Last chord played,
she turns
waves farewell with *that* walk
and leaves on my arm.

Warning Signs

*Last week, days were hot, clouds gone
and all that could be done, was.
My share of the world was generous.
Yesterday the sun warmed my back
as I soared on the false wind of a manic day.
This morning it caught the twinkle in my eye
and pearled sweat on my forehead by lunch.
Liberal in its favours,
these treats I assumed were everyone's ...*

... until late in the afternoon
when that same sun set suddenly on me,
in exclusivity,
leaving me in that awful twilight zone,
that grey announcement
warning of the eclipse.

I know
this thing.
I live with
this thing.
It damages
this thing.

Despite all I know of this enemy,
despite all I can do ,
once it storms my mental ramparts
I can only turn it back,
I can never stop it coming.

Fear holds hands with that thought
for I have known days
when I was its ragged puppet
and death - whilst not a victory -
offered at least relief.

Days of no sunrise,
no corner to cower in.
My mind was not mine
but then,
madness is no hiding place.

As the greyness deepens
I'll do what I have to
and beat back the intruder again.
Fear prickling me with incentive
and the price of failure.

This poem was first published on the website of
the Black Dog Institute.

Safe Harbour

In that space, afterwards, before sleep,
you hold me, cradled in your scent,
nuzzling me to your warmth, your softness
and entwined in arms like silken cords.

You talk of my angularity,
the constancy of muscle and bone.
To you I am all strength and perseverance
and courage and durability.

You talk of love.
There, safe in your harbour
and tied securely to your mooring,
how can I disagree.

It's here I have hidden from storms,
protected from one point agendas
with my name on them.
Meetings closed, I'm hiding still.

Broken and torn then,
plastered, painted and papered now,
I'm still a scared old lion
footsore from the yellow brick road.

Wrapped in your cosy envelope,
I'm both strength and vulnerability.
Believing I can but fearing I can't
and scared of the world outside your arms.

Words replaced by your steady, sleeping breath,
I answer only my own thoughts.
Tears brink as a lithium shake
rocks me gently into sleep.

I'll be braver tomorrow.

Change of Days
(camping at Yamba)

Soft restlessness of leaves
canvas walls flap a sporadic flush of air
persistent singing of unseen insects
faithful cars shepherd drunken rams home
distant rumbling and roaring of an unconcerned ocean
"G-day" mumbled to a neon silhouette
strange conversations with a wandering radio dial
a country singer silenced by a key turn
gravel complaining of a heavy load
water spills, rested loose from canvas pools by the wind
urine spills, rested loose from a brinked bladder
big talk from drunken boys
small talk from drunken men
rustling nylon and long zip, zip, zippers
the rush of water to the boil
clanking spoons on enamel pannikins
and the "r" in hot coffee
insistent urging bettered by adamant refusal
a Ford clicks, screams and slams its door
then winks twice at any bystanders
farts,
giggles,
more farts,
banishment

Noisiest of all
an unquiet mind
recording these secrets
I relight my pipe
and listen
as soft restlessness comes again

That Mate Of Mine

Nice day
Nice suit
Nice tie
Nice shoes
You've never looked so good
You've never looked so calm.
They've all come to see you.
Blokes in four ironed creases,
sharp ties.
Ladies in wicked posh frocks,
new stockings.
We'll talk a lot today.
Talk about you.
Laugh at roguish antics.
Hide faces at times
when facades falter,
'till we have those few beers
and politely eat sandwiches
and colour our conversations
monochrome in front of grandmas.
You'd love this day,
painted on a family palette
with it's catching up,
the spreading of bulldust
pungent in men's laughter.
The beers, the jokes, the tears,
the mates ...

      ... too many beers ...

          ... dishes and a dirty bbq ...

... tomorrow's problem ...

... late night sporting highlights ...

... a couple pf lonely whiskies ...

... just my echoes against the walls ...

... I missed you today.
Wished makeup on another face.
and someone else dead
wearing your suit.
I willed a smile from you
which never came.
Told you my best punchline,
which you finally ignored
and hours later,
guests reteated,
I've just realised you're gone.
I should have treasured you
in quiet moments men dread.
You are gone,
so I'll take loneliness to the footy
and wait for it to shout.
Cry my tears
in safe places
and practice saying your name
to adjust to the pain it brings.
If I bend my back and shovel
I might just fill the hole you've left,
ten minutes before I join you.

News Day

Morning.
He feels the stirrings of old ways and means
liquid steel runs into places
too soft for too long
He can sniff the winds of change
see the brand as it turns in approach
He is ready
He will compete
He will honour the men
of this family
but this time
with no grass stains
or torn hamstrings
or weakness.
Today he brings best gifts to the table

Midday.
The waiting starts
The sound of time ticking
only heard when each screw
is bedded
each nail tired of abuse
from a hammer's rusty swings.
In the silence of brewed tea
he wonders on the news
the afternoon lingers to.
He knows.
Has known for weeks
Tricked himself into hope
and rings again and again
until his father finds a voice.

Late Afternoon.
He hears the rumble
of Auden's distant thunder
at a picnic
and though he knows it comes
he doesn't know how fast.
So it is with death.
Tonight he'll wet himself with tears
in anticipation of the storm's work
and wait and watch
as a great one slips from his grasp.
The task,
to fill each moment with gratitude
and the hope of what might yet be done
with these lessons learned.

Evening.
He sobs
at the myth of immortality
and the fear of loneliness.
He cries
not for past lost chances
but for future opportunities.
He moans
for conversations treasured
and those to be missed.
He screams
at God
for these final cruelties
and shakes and shakes and shakes
in acceptance.

Finding Home

They watched me stand tall,
speak words for you
and laugh at your life and times
and remarked my strength,
named by you, The Rock.
I made it so easy to disbelieve belief,
gave grief a time plausibility
explained the opportunity for goodbyes
and the inevitability of plans made
as though your death was on my itinerary.

Then Santa bought me presents:
almost all who cause my smile
sat about my tree,
ate at my table,
laughed, cried and loved each other.
You were there with them
holding their hearts,
nursing bruises and making it right.
But in my house,
I knew the hiding places

so I hid in illness
and other mysteries,
but my control slips away
now the house is empty
and shadows have names
and intentions.
Grief waits for me in the visitor's room,
in a wardrobe full of Hawaiian shirts.
Bright colours and good times
and an old lady dancing.

My heart will break soon,
not soon enough,
a deluge of salty tears
and the grinding of everything broken
heart, mind and soul
Out Of Order.
Haunted, I wake shivering,
terrified at control handed over
even in such a just cause.
Can I return if I go there?

Top End Morning

Pre dawn arrives again about my bed
The ceiling yields to greys then yellows
as rogue stars twinkle last greetings.
Last night at first light.
I dismiss a falling star
and leave wishes with a rising sun.
Birds sing some comfort
urging patience I can't find
for a night I'm done with.
Stealing blankets with each toss,
stealing sleep in turns.
Coaxing cuddles till she rolls away
to her own dreams.
Counting hours
for permission to wake.
Sweating on a noisy neighbour
starting his morning dedications
to a wife who craves tea and toast.
The first walkers pass my flyscreened feet,
New Balanced and Just Doing It.
A ticket of leave
to my own cup of tea,
a pen,
a blank page
and her last hour of sleep.
I long-zip a doorway onto the morning
and jangled nerves jangle ideas instead.
Near naked and totally exposed
a top end morning washes me clean,
flushing the night from my soul
until hope runs in my pen.
I was raised for such mornings
and live every moment it offers.
Soon she will stir
and smile thirty years past a tent pole
and a better day will best itself.

Little Amiss

I miss your soft smiles
more than your hard nipples.
I miss your dry humour
more than your moist invitation.
I miss your confident personality
more than your shy nudity.
I miss your short laugh
more than your long legs.
I miss your small comments
more than your large breasts.
I miss watching you dance
more than watching you dress.
I miss your surprises
more than your disappointments.
I miss what you give me
more than what I give you.
I miss you making me full
more than me making us empty.
I miss your mysteries
more than your explanations.
I miss taking your hand
more than taking advantage.
I miss seeing you create
more than owning your creation.
I miss your cooking
more than your groceries.
I even miss your singing.

I miss you,
not your parts.

That Coldest Hour

Lying here at your cold shoulder,
your decisions made for both of us,
I often marvel at the strength and resolve
survival has gifted you
and taken from me,
but realise too soon,
I am not the only one damaged by your strength.

You've lost that little girl
who once played with your imagination,
evolving to a teenage flirt
still wide-eyed with possibilities.
Angry with the world
whilst loving everyone in it.

When did responsibility show her the door?
When did practicality wave to her from the window?
When did common sense become common?
What did I do
to get you into caveman pelts
and have you bare your teeth
in grim survival?

By comparison,
that cold stare speared into my side
or jagged comment held to my throat
seems a lesser penalty …
but then, you have menopause,
I've only got madness.

Lying here at your cold shoulder,
both of us safely behind shields –
me in the wake of my Lithium droop
and you walled in by feminine hygiene –
I'm suddenly glad it's Friday.

Saturday's are always happier.

Non Scholae Sed Vitae

Sitting on the last of your nineteen steps
a concrete column supporting eaves and I,
both of us disclosing grey lines I'll call experience.
I share your north-faced view
for only moments of your steadfast seventy year vigil
and wonder would you notice me less,
quietly sitting here in my crowd of one
or when I rose on other's shoulders,
desperate for attention.

Armidale, as winter relinquishes to spring.
Skies whose only break in continuity is the changing hue
from deep blue infinity where it hurts your neck to look
down to the shallow near-white stuff
hugging hills and tree lines
and the occasional unnatural silhouette.
Lower still, closer to view,
drought defying green,
in shades to yellow,
a concession to thirst.

At your concrete feet all cracked and patched and scarred
from that marriage of too much time and too little care,
from that space where learning began ...
roses lay in waiting, longing for a spring escape.
Perhaps a thousand thorny fingers
have published small notices of intention.
Flags of all colours offer safe landing
and friendship for bees and visitors of trade.
Pansies wave their own welcome
calling out in a host of colourful voices:
purples, yellows, reds, whites and more purples.

Armidale Teachers College she will always be.
Those hunger-fed on votes may change her name,
without our votes cast,
but even these party-masked thieves
will never steal her identity.
Here on the hill, still facing north,
her eyes never once blinking at the bright sun,
yet winking at the bright daughters and sons

shaped not for learning but for living
in her shelter.
In this moment, she shines as always.

Standing back, I see what Drummond dreamed
and Smith saw in convict blocks.
Nineteen steps, six columns and a winking door,
beckoning me,
drawing me,
welcoming me home.
Thirty years and a life lived my way later,
I still remember three years
as moments in technicolour.
I smell the rain.
I shiver in the winter cold.
I feel the stabs of a lover's spurning.
I taste the sweetness of a lover found.
I touch the future, now as then.

I am still learning.
I am living.

Afterword

It has been both a pleasure and a privilege to come to know Peter Langston and his remarkable poetry. Peter's is a poetic voice which is unique in the freshness of the language, the creativity of the imagery and the bold architectonic of structure, which gives well-worn themes rejuvenated expression, so transformational as to suggest the arrival of a new apocalyptic vision on the horizon.

Authentically new voices in poetry are always rare but Peter Langston produces inspiring innovation: this is exemplified in "That Coldest Hour", a magnificently crafted poem which is an incisive analysis of how he carved the world view out of exploring the dialectic of his marriage;

> Lying there at your cold shoulder,
> Both of us safely behind shields -
> Me in the wake of my Lithium droop
> And you walled in by feminine hygiene,
> I'm suddenly glad it is Friday.
> Saturday's are always happier.

The power of the poetry is in the recognition that compassionate understanding must go beyond personal suffering to extend to the realization that emotional trauma is reciprocal and must be accepted as both a grace and a burden.

This is one of the most moving and technically accomplished poems I have read in the last decade.

But apart from his intensely personal poetry, which is nakedly confessional, Peter also writes what one might call "public poetry" in which he comments, sometimes satirically but always incisively on the human condition at large.

To give two examples, in "His Favourite Chair", the emptying of a dwelling's furniture records:

> Carefully, they hid his medals
> Beneath his parent's gold framed wedding,
> Beneath a drawer from her craft room,
> Beneath three toilet rolls and a work jumper.
> Their life recorded by a stranger's priorities
> and vouched safe to ribbed cardboard
> and screaming tape.
> Each yelp a newly-stabbed pain.

and finally raises the epistemological question: "what, at its end, is a life worth?" The answer seems to be: "It's all about sanitizing—everything can be packed into a box and disposed of, except perhaps the widow's grief which screams with the tape, although being subdued by middle-class conventions is, paradoxically, almost silent."

In "Chocos", there is a sharp and acerbic black humoured comment:

> General Blame-Me
> Of firm footing and starched uniform,
> both testicles in Macarthur's hand
> and kicking own goals with his mouth,
> dismissed their effort.

It is my view that the private and public poems of Peter Langston are inseparably integrated: Peter's observation creates his poetry and reciprocally, his poetry creates a world in which he can find, if not paradise, then secular sanctuary in which he can resolve his existential angst and come to terms with both his personal life and his relationship to the world at large.

The final comment which needs to be made about Peter's poetry is that it never meanders into saccharine whimsy: it always and sometimes aggressively, embraces stark imaginative truth.

Finally, Peter's poetry is elemental: an intellectual and emotional verbal display, which stretches as far back as when the first hominids learned to differentiate between vowels and consonants and dared to unleash the crafted passion of raw emotion.

I look forward to many more volumes of Peter's poetry.

Barry Richardson

B.A., B. Leg.S, M.Litt, M.A. Solicitor of the Supreme Court of N.S.W., Sometime Lecturer in English and Cultural Studies, ACAE and UNE.

Sadly, Barry has not lived to see this second edition, having fallen quickly to cancer not long enough after his guiding hand helped me deliver the original. His generosity to me was no more than that which he extended throughout his teaching career, with great passion and total commitment. I will always be grateful for his kind words and wise counsel. (PL)

Dedication

No writer ever acts alone: whether it be his muse, characters he meets, family and friends or just the lady at the paper shop with the lovely smile, writers are surrounded by sources.

I have been a writer almost as far back as I can remember and a voiceless poet until recently. I would like to thank the many people who have surrounded me ... and the list has grown longer since this book was first published, such is my uncanny luck! Bear with me please, but I need to thank:

- Paul & Jan McManus, of Collins Booksellers (Tamworth & Armidale), who support local poets generally but me in particular, by providing an outlet for my books and the opportunity to showcase them when they are launched;

- Kelly Fuller, Anna Moulder and Jen Ingle of ABC New England North West, for their support of the Arts and willingness to given an unknown a go;

- Emelia Saban, for the opportunity she opened up and her faith in my work;

- Eric Bogle, for the inspiration to be better each time I write and to know that to stop caring is to stop living;

- every mongrel who has caused me grief and every person with a kind smile- you have all been of enormous help;

- Mrs Church, Mrs Fox, Miss Fisk, Mr Deane: teachers who used their candle to light mine. John Rummery and Barry Richardson: teachers who recognised my light;

- my big sister Lesley and all the musicians I have channelled to gain such a rich musical education;

- John Hildred, Peter Quirk, Andrew Davis, Tony Bennett and Claude Orenstein - the truest of friends, who offered acceptance as the best way to express their love;

- my children, Chris, Sarah and Sam who have allowed me to both teach and learn from them and have never given up on me, even after earning the right to;

- my brother Art, who never quits, especially on me. He's been there at all the crucial moments, lending me strength, wisdom and courage. I'm often breathing his air. I love you Arty.

- God ... what can I say? Very clever guy. Good planner. Sneaky ... and a wonderful sense of irony. Just as well <u>he</u> knew what he was doin'.

- my Dad, my cornerstone, who taught me that manhood, included crying when you are sad <u>and</u> when you are happy and then hung around to provide me with advice and friendship, despite the cost. I have known no better man than him . I bear his mark proudly;

- my remarkable best friend, Sue, whom I have written about in light and shade. She's not perfect but the difference is such a small margin of tolerance you couldn't machine it. Thank you for never thinking "the inbetweens would ever fall away"[1]. Thank you for revival when I was exhausted. Thank you for fighting to be you. A second thank you to God for arranging the intro.

Finally, this book is dedicated to all but none of you as I got this gift a long time ago and was nurtured through sacrifice and encouragement even though the giver had no idea what her genes had unleashed. These 42 poems - my life of meaning - are dedicated to June Langston, my mum, who gave me life from start to finish and sent me out to be her dreamer - an instruction I intend to obey until I join her.

Thanks Mum, you old dag.

---

1. From "Better Day" by Chris Langston

Poet's Notes
The Title - is a Douglas Adams reference. In one of my favourite books, 'Hitchhiker's Guide to the Galaxy', the incorrect equation 6 x 9 = 42 is a key story point. When I realised I had 42 poems to publish, the title seemed obvious. For the Sheldons who have immediately gone to the contents page and counted, the notes about Page 36 should sate your objections.
Page 5 - a love poem to my wife written on or about our 25th wedding anniversary
Page 6 - written on the southern headland of Coogee beach. The wildness of the ocean and stubborn resistance of the headland reminded me of the relationship with my daughter. The poem is a statement of acceptance and pride.
Page 8 - first drafted the night of my youngest son's graduation as a teacher and reflecting on the previous four years of his life.
Page 9 - I had always identified with Peter Pan as a boy (okay, for some time after that). When I was mentally unwell, I determined to 'find my happy thought' and it became the thought of a time in the future when I would hold my eldest son's son for the first time.
Page 10 - observed this scene in the flat next door to my son's as an elderly woman was being moved after the sudden death of her husband of more than fifty years.
Page 12 - observations from a Anzac Day dawn service, standing behind a bunch of Vietnam vets in biker's colours.
Pages 14&15 - two poems for my Mum, who loved doing two things: playing piano and gardening.
Page 16 - my wife was the 4th child of five who were raised on a dairy farm on an island in the Lower Clarence Valley and for nine years she was the youngest and subject to the privileges that entailed.
Page 18 - dreaming about the one you love when you are separated by great distance
Page 19 - in the depths of depression, leaving the house was extremely difficult. The daily shopping list was my wife's act of love in helping me meet that challenge.
Page 20 - this poem grew from two lines which had rattled about my head for months 'I shut my eyes for sleep, a coward's suicide"
Page 21 - written at sunset at Windjana Gorge, in the Kimberley of WA. We were out of contact range with Dad, knowing full well that Mum was in her last days. As I sat alone in the gorge watching the sunset, she was with me.
Page 22 - the story of Maroubra Force, the untrained rabble of reservists who slowed the Japanese progress toward Port Moresby over the Kokoda Track in 1942, long enough for the professional soldiers to arrive and were then heavily criticised by Australian and Allied commanders.
Page 24 - a gathering of old mates in their forties, facing change and supporting each other.
Page 26 - four girls who were like a throw back to past times.
Page 28 - my first grandchild, August, lost at ten weeks.
Page 29 - looking at the face of a two year old.
Page 30&31 - two poems about my wife: the first at a Countdown revival concert where 18 months of hard weight loss work was squeezed into new jeans and the second about the price I had to pay in order for weight loss program to succeed.

Page 32 - a simple catalogue poem constructed while drinking coffee outside the supermarket.
Page 34 - anyone with insomnia born of depression knows this routine.
Page 35 - another poem built from two lines, spoken to a doctor, after months of tests to determine causes 'too sick to live, too well to die'.
Page 36 - this started as two poems about the same box of diverse keep sakes of my mothers. The first was a recollection of her trying to sort through them and bring order (the left hand side) and the second about me looking into the box some time after she died (the right hand side).
Page 38 - I stopped at the Royal Hotel, Spring Ridge, late one afternoon on the way home to Tamworth from Canberra.
Page 40 - a poem for two voices (one reads the "singing" line) based on the memory of meeting my wife, for the first time, in a wine bar in Armidale.
Page 45 - a poem written about the behind the counter bloke at the Nullarbor Roadhouse: a man of few words and who knows what thoughts, he was the spitting image of Rowan Atkinson's Mr Bean.
Page 46 - this poem stemmed from my wife's comment in Lightening Ridge that everything appeared broken and became a homage to Bob Dylan's "Everything Is Broken".
Page 47 - a true story of a night out with a mate's band of 'experienced' rock campaigners. Much of the audience were similarly experienced, except for a crew of pimply uni students in the corner. It all came unstuck when a middle aged goddess took to the floor to dance and became the centre of attention.
Page 50 - intended to highlight the rapid changes of mood which can affect a person with bipolar disorder.
Page 52 - a poem about vulnerability and the bulwark that unconditional love can provide against it.
Page 53 - one of the few surviving poems worth keeping from early twenties. Another catalogue poem.
Page 54 - how men grieve.
Page 56 - a long day waiting for news of tests to determine if my father had cancer.
Page 58 - a poem that spans four months, from the eulogy I gave at my mother's funeral to Christmas Day and how I tried to cope with her death.
Page 59 - a love poem, also drafted first at Windjana Gorge. It describes both my love for my wife and a key coping strategy when I am depressed: watching the sunrise and recalibrating.
Page 60 - this is the result of too much red wine, the lateness of the hour and someone you love insisting on being given details of why you love them.
Page 61 - written in capitals in the online convention of shouting, it portrays the unreasonable and dangerous nature of anger and honesty when mixed in haste during the short course of argument.
Page 62 - a perfect example of the assertion by the French poet, Paul Valery, who said "a poem is never finished, only abandoned". I have worked this poem more often than any other, only to abandon it again and again, unfinished. In editing this 2nd edition, I considered removing it, but retained it only to keep the title of the book true to its origin. It will likely remain unfinished.

www.ingramcontent.com/pod-product-compliance
Lightning Source LLC
Chambersburg PA
CBHW071414040426
42444CB00009B/2238